"Cézanne has only to lay in one dab of colour; it is nothing and it is beautiful."

Auguste Renoir

He was "... a big solid youth standing on rather slender legs. He walked with an even step, head held high as if he were looking at the horizon. His noble face, framed by a curly beard, recalled the figures of the Assyrian gods ... He normally had a serious expression, but when he spoke, his features became animated and an expressive mimicry accompanied his words which he uttered with a strong well-timbred voice." This was how the critic Georges Rivière described Cézanne in 1870.

Paul Cézanne was born in Aix-en-Provence on January 10th, 1839, into a comfortable middle-class family. His father, the owner of a hat-making company, had rescued a bank in financial difficulties. This had made him a rich man. Paul had followed a classical course of studies at his school in Aix and there he developed a strong friendship with the future writer Emile Zola. He went on to study literature and law at the local university. However, he did not complete his studies; his passion for painting became too strong to leave room for any other interests. His whole life centred around his art and neither the social events of the times, nor the Franco-Prussian War in 1870, nor the tormented politics which took place during his lifetime, nor even his own family circumstances had any effect on him. His life was bound up by his work and it permitted no distractions from the continuous act of creation. Comparing himself to an almond tree that gives unstintingly of its fruit in due season, Cézanne recognised an inner, almost biological, compulsion that made his painting a vital act.

His family, traditional and rather puritanical, at first was worried by his choice of vocation, which seemed to them a risky one. But they eventually resigned themselves to it and, wishing to protect the young Cézanne from the hazards of life as a poor struggling artist, they provided him with the means to work comfortably without financial worries. They removed all obstacles and made no demands that he earn a living. The allowance his family gave him permitted him to live with great dignity and the inheritance he received on his father's death not only relieved him from any financial worries whatsoever, but also released him from the often tyrannical demands of dealers and buyers.

Under the tutelage of the master Joseph Gilbert, the young Cézanne learned the rudiments of painting at the School of Fine Arts in Aix-en-Provence. His ambition, like those of many artists living in the provinces, was to go to Paris. His childhood friend Emile Zola, had moved there, and Zola strongly urged Cézanne to join him. Paul Cézanne's first visit to the capital was made when he was twenty-two. He spent six months there, from April to September 1861. He left disillusioned. After admiring the masterpieces of the great masters in the Louvre and attending the Salon, held during his stay, Paul returned to Aix discouraged by his progress and doubting his talent. In a letter written to his friend Baille dated June 10th, 1861, Emile Zola described Cézanne in a way that revealed Zola's complete lack of understanding of the artist and deeply wounded Cézanne. Zola wrote: "He is a solid piece, obdurate and hard, nothing bends him, nothing can drag a concession from him. If by chance he puts forth some mistaken idea and I argue with him, he loses his temper without even listening to what has been said, he tells you that you don't know anything about it and quickly changes the subject." (Zola persisted in seeing Cézanne as an "abortive genius" and a "failure", and years later he described the hero, the painter Lantier, in his work *L'Oeuvre* in a similar fashion; Cézanne, recognising himself in the portrait, was deeply offended.) That same year, 1861, Cézanne wrote: "The sky of my future is completely black" and he accepted a job in his father's bank. However, his passion for painting refused to die, and, denied admission into the School of Fine Arts in Paris, Cézanne worked instead at the Académie Suisse, a private studio near Notre-Dame. He also submitted work to the Salon during that period but he was refused. This lack of official acceptance was to continue for many

The Large Bathers - 1875-76. National Gallery, London

3

years; Cézanne was often to suffer the incomprehension of the public as well as the critics and dealers. Even as late as the 1920's, the curator of the museum at Aix-en-Provence declared that he was happy he did not own any of the master's works and he hoped the museum would not be offered any.

During the Franco-Prussian War in 1870, Cézanne, who had very little interest in politics and feared any trouble that might prevent him from carrying on his work, moved to L'Estaque, a village near the sea, west of Marseille, where his mother had some property. Cézanne, writing to Pissarro in 1876, described the countryside as "like a playing card. Red roofs on a blue sea. The sun is so strong that the objects seem to stand out in silhouette, not only in black and white, but in blue, red, brown and violet." He returned to Paris only after the last guns were silenced.

During the years that followed, the painter alternated his stays in Paris with long periods of meditation in Aix for he had a savage need for independence, endlessly repeating with a rough eloquence that he would never "let them get their hooks" into him. When he was in the capital, he would go to the literary cafés, the Guerbois in particular, in the Grand-Rue des Batignolles, and there he met such Impressionists as Monet, Bazille, Renoir, Sisley, Guillaumin and Manet. The Batignolle painters had decided to form a new group, the "Société Anonyme Coopérative des Artistes Peintres, Sculpteurs et Graveurs", in opposition to the Salon. As part of this group, Cézanne showed thirty of his paintings for the first time, at an exhibition held in the studio of the photographer Nadar at 35 Boulevard des Capucines from April 15th to May 15th, 1874. Yet the new Impressionist techniques did not completely satisfy him. "I would like to make of Impressionism something solid and durable like the art of museums", he said and he remained, in some senses, distanced from the movement by his aesthetics. In any case the importance he gave to "sensations" was very different from the purely visual effects of the true Impressionists. Emile Bernard was correct when he said that "far from being spontaneous, Cézanne is deliberate. His genius is a flash that goes deep. I have no qualms in affirming that Cézanne is a painter with a mystical temperament ... because of his purely abstract and aesthetic vision of things." Sensation was important to him: "Sensation" said Cézanne "is the basis of everything for the painter"; to the poet Joachim Gasquet, he said: "Yes, I want to know: to know, the better to feel; to feel, the better to know. I want to be a true classical painter, to become classical through nature." That same year, 1874, in the gentle countryside of the Île-de-France, the famous meeting took place between Cézanne and Pissarro, whom the artist from Provence always considered "something like God the Father". Pissarro often told him: "Paint only with the three primary colours and their immediate derivatives", a lesson that Cézanne would not ignore.

At their third group exhibition in 1877 Cézanne again exhibited with the Impressionists, but he ran up against a confused public and narrow-minded critics. However, as time went on, he began to exhibit with more success. In 1890 his works were shown in Brussels with a group called "Les Vingt". In 1895 he participated in a group exhibition organised by Vollard, who recognised the value of his work and strongly believed in his art. At that same exhibition Gustave Geffroy, of whom Cézanne had painted a masterly portrait, said of the artist: "He will go to the Louvre", a prophecy that was not long in coming true. In 1898 and 1899 Cézanne was invited to participate in the Salon des Indépendants, and in 1900, at the large Centennial Exhibition, his canvases were included in a retrospective of French art.

At last the public began to understand and appreciate Cézanne. He became a regular exhibitor at the Salon des Indépendants where he again showed his work in 1901 and 1902. In 1904 at the Salon d'Automne, a whole room was devoted to his canvases.

In October 1904 a tired and unwell Cézanne was working outside as usual, when he was caught in a sudden and violent storm on the road to Thonolet near Sainte-Victoire. He collapsed. He was taken home to Rue Boulegnon by the driver of a laundry cart who found him lying unconscious along the road. Cézanne was confined to bed but he continued to be obsessed until the day he died with the idea of not leaving any canvas unfinished. A few days later, on October 22nd, he died of pulmonary congestion. It had been his greatest wish to die working.

Cézanne's is an example of a life haunted by a single passion. Art is a jealous mistress to whom everything must be sacrificed and existence is expressed only through work, which becomes its sole object. It was characteristic of Cézanne that on the day of his mother's funeral he went out painting, instead of, as is usual, attending the ceremony. He did not do this from lack of feeling or from ignorance of what was proper; it was simply, for him, the greatest homage he could pay his mother.

Cézanne was a man with a single vocation and he pursued it in spite of changes of politics, metaphysics or love. There were few women in his life apart from his mother and his wife Hortense Fiquet, whom he married after she gave birth to their son Paul.

On Sundays he attended Mass at the cathedral of Saint-Sauveur; his spiritual life extended no further than that.

No real clue, then, is offered to us which would allow us to explain the reality of Cézanne's myth. Kurt Badt, who more than any other painter, was able to express the depth of Cézanne's thoughts and works, said: "In certain paintings by Cézanne, his personal experiences come to light in more or less disguised form and I find myself compelled to see and interpret his art from this particular angle, primarily because of its subjective aspects. The result has been that his work appeared to me like a great *confession*, like the works of Goethe and Delacroix, of Stendhal and Flaubert, of Stifter and Caspar David Friedrich and its starting point, in the characteristic manner of the 19th century, lays in the artist's suffering and his victory over that suffering."

But there is also in his work "the melancholy of Provence that no one has described", as Cézanne confided one day to Gasquet. A melancholy that Maurice Brion called *romantic-expressionist*. Gasquet one day questioned Emile Zola, Cézanne's friend from his youth, about that dash of romanticism. Zola confirmed that "from his childhood he was furious about the romantic gangrene that he possessed. It was his malady, perhaps the false idea that one sometimes carries like a millstone around the neck." That period Cézanne called his *couillarde* period, meaning vigorous, bold, hearty, or daring. Not yet constrained by the rigid discipline that he imposed on himself later, Cézanne gave free rein during this period to his violent youthful temperament. The inner turmoil he felt, controlled and expressed in the opposite concepts of colour and form, is reflected in his work *The Thieves and the Donkey* (also called *Sancho Panza*) and again in *The Orgy* and *Afternoon in Naples*. It can also be seen in *A Modern Olympia*, one version of which is in the Lecomte collection and another version painted by Cézanne in 1873-74, several years later, is in the Musée d'Orsay. They are compositions full of "brio" where touches of colour fall in a rapid cascade.

During his *couillarde* period, even in pictures of simple design such as *The Negro Scipio* and *The Penitent Magdalen* the immobility of the sitter is compensated by the sheer expressive power of the paint. For Cézanne, a portrait was nothing but a certain arrangement of lines, volumes and colour, as in *Achille Emperaire* or *Uncle Dominique*, a portrait of his mother's brother whom he painted twice, once dressed as a monk and once as a lawyer. These are canvases where the paint is piled on in a thick impasto, portraits that leave no room for psycho-

Cézanne

PARK
LANE

Schools Library and Information Service

logical analysis, this "strange paradox" as Guerry points out in *Cézanne et l'impression de l'espace* regarding the painting *Stove in the Studio* : "While the young girl at the piano and her companion have the immobility of inanimate objects, the stove, the kettle and the clock rise before us like living things. If it were not held down by a heavy cauldron, the stove with its elaborate feet, would soon be moving towards us like a spiritualist's table at a seance."

Attracted by the poetry of familiar everyday objects, Cézanne followed the examples of the Spanish and Dutch schools, paying attention to "the silent life of things". The changeover from the animate to the inanimate, and back again was an operation dependent on pure painting.

The landscapes from that period are outstanding: *Factory near Mont Sainte-Victoire, Melting Snow at L'Estaque* or *The Railway Cut*, a true masterpiece about which Guerry, in the text mentioned previously, said: "The device of using screens which Cézanne was apt to place too abruptly in canvases contemporaneous with this one, results in a flawless rhythmic pattern, thanks to an admirable intuitive sense of the necessary balancings and compensations."

His way of seeing grew simpler and he painted an admirable *Fishing Village at L'Estaque*, a painting more classically beautiful, according to Cézanne's definition of the word. Cézanne confided to Gasquet that he loved these landscapes: "The great classical landscapes, our Provence, Greece and Italy such as I imagine them, are those where light is spiritual, where a landscape is a smile flickering with keen intelligence."

And so he was ready to approach Impressionism, but always in his own way, one very different from that of Monet, Renoir or Sisley. Following the advice of Pissarro, his palette grew lighter, and his technique changed. He began to work using small dabs of colour, juxtaposing and superimposing them until he achieved the effect he desired. He studied the variations of colour and the play of light on objects, preferring to work with his favourite motif of the moment, vases of flowers (*Delftware Vase with Flowers, Geraniums in a Pot, Vase with Tulips*) which L. Guerry explained by the fact that, "searching to express an atmospheric unity, he was afraid that this unity would be compromised if there were too violent a contrast between the object and space."

Pissarro, meanwhile, insisted that Cézanne should paint only in the open air; outside, the variations of light were greater and his canvases would gain an Impressionistic freshness that work inside the studio would inhibit.

In 1872 he was back at work in Pontoise, and in 1873 and 1874 he went to Auvers-sur-Oise where Pissarro lived. It was during this period that he painted his second *A Modern Olympia* — inspired by Manet's painting in 1863 — a painting whose spirit was still romantic, but whose technique was now undeniably Impressionist. The watercolour *Lutte d'Amour, Temptations of Saint Anthony, Luncheon on the Grass* and the aforementioned *The Thieves and the Donkey* (or *Sancho Panza*) were also painted during this period. His first studies of *Bathers*, a theme that would dominate his large canvases between 1900 and 1905, date from his stay in Auvers-sur-Oise. There would eventually be forty-two variations on this theme, not to mention numerous sketches.

In 1877 he painted the portrait of a customs official, Victor Chocquet, in bold strong tones, and an austere portrait *Madame Cézanne Sewing*, in which the figure seems to blend into the background, her essence caught forever. In the portrait *Self-Portrait with Pink Spots*, the pink spots on the wall are "conceived as a necessary accompaniment, vital to the cohesion of the different elements that make up Cézanne's appearance, forming an almost identical replica of his face. The light pink clouds on a grey ground even pass over his face, breaking it up into lighter and darker zones, and giving it a changing

Ruined House - 1892-94. Private collection, USA

touchy expression" (Guerry). The process for *Self-Portrait with Hat* is the same: the figure is integrated into the surroundings, the face is set, the inanimate becomes animate. However *Self-Portrait with a Cap*, painted around the same time, seems to retain something of the earlier romantic-expressionist period of the artist.

The most famous works from the time he spent in Auvers-sur-Oise are *The House of Père Lacroix*, the three versions of *Doctor Gachet's House* and *Snow Effect near Auvers*. Even though they avoid the "atomization" of light which characterises the works of Monet, they are undeniably Impressionist in style. In another work, *The Poplars*, painted during that period, the trees reflect the vibrancy of light and wind while preserving their austere immutability.

Certainly, however, the most famous painting from his Impressionist period was *Hanged Man's House* which he completed in 1873. Its technique is innovative. Under Pissarro's influence, Cézanne's palette had grown lighter, and sombre tones (influenced by such masters as Delacroix, Daumier and Courbet) were replaced by more luminous colours, although he continued to use a thickly-coated brush and even at times a spatula knife. Cézanne worked with juxtaposed strokes of colour in the Impressionist manner, but the structure of his tableau was a confirmation of his desire for a rigorous almost architectural construction of space. The canvas also represented a change in his choice of subjects. Cézanne henceforth abandoned the dramatic literary themes he had previously used and turned to insignificant objects that would take on meaning through the artist's interpretation of them. *Hanged Man's House*, the fruit of an Impressionism reinterpreted and transformed by Cézanne, was exhibited by the artist at the Centenary of French Art at the Paris World's Fair which opened in 1889 in the

Champ-de-Mars to celebrate the Revolution of 1789. However, the first time it had been displayed, at the Impressionist exhibition of 1874, it had been very badly received. In his memoires, Paul Durand-Ruel, the art dealer in Rue Laffitte who had been a champion of the Impressionist artists, recounts: "The public came in droves, but with their minds made up beforehand; they saw in these great artists only presumptuous fools trying to gain attention by their eccentricities. There was a wave of opinion against them and great hilarity, contempt and even indignation that permeated every circle, every studio, salon and even the theatres, where they were held up to ridicule." Though he lived simply, the allowance Cézanne received from his father at the time was not always enough to cover his needs. At one point, Cézanne was forced to try to earn some money by selling his paintings at a group auction organised by other Impressionists, among them Berthe Morisot, Sisley, Renoir and Monet. The sale was held on March 25th, 1875 at the Hôtel Drouot. It was a disaster. In the newspaper *Figaro*, the critic Albert Wolff referred to the artists as "monkeys who had got hold of palettes". In 1876 a second Impressionist exhibition was held at the gallery of Durand-Ruel. It was another fiasco. However, although the Parisian public remained hostile to a form of painting it did not understand, certain critics began to defend this revolutionary art. In 1877 great battles raged around the third Impressionist exhibition in Rue Peletier. Cézanne himself exhibited seventeen canvases, but unfortunately they did not enjoy any great success. The critic Leroy of *Charivari* warned visitors not to show a pregnant woman Cézanne's portrait of Chocquet: "The head, painted the colour of the inside of a boot, is so strange that the impression it might produce could cause yellow fever in the fruit of her womb before its arrival into this world."

But Georges Rivière, an employee of the Ministry of Finance and an art critic, replied in his paper *Impressionniste*: "Cézanne is a painter and a great one at that ... His still lifes, so beautiful and so exact in their tonal relations, have something solemn about them in their truthfulness. In all his paintings, the artist moves us, because he himself feels such strong emotion when confronted with nature and he transmits this to the canvas." He goes on to warn the public about "imperfections which are in fact a refinement obtained through great skill."

After the exhibition of Rue Peletier, Cézanne wanting "to be freed from the beasts", moved permanently to Provence. There he began the second phase of his career, his so-called *constructive* period, in which he intended to "treat nature according to the sphere, the cylinder and the cone, with everything put into perspective so that each side of an object or a plane is aimed towards a central point." This statement has led some critics to consider him the father of Cubism.

Without rejecting anything that he had assimilated previously in his *couillarde* period or that he had learned from Pissarro, Cézanne moved away from Impressionism. Even though he preserved certain techniques of that movement, he used his new-found freedom to imagine new spatial relationships different from traditional perspective. This progression was made without breaks or ruptures, in perfect harmony with nature, which "makes no leap", the culmination of an infinite number of steps. As one period ended and another began, certain existing tendencies in his painting were maintained and others were discarded. In a letter to Emile Bernard of July 25th, 1904, Cézanne described his quest: "For progress to be made, there is only nature and the eye must be educated to it. It becomes concentric by continually looking and working. What I mean is that in an orange, an apple, a ball, a head, there is a culminating point; and that point is always — in spite of the terrible effect of light and shadow, of colour sensations — the one closest to our eye. The edges of objects recede towards a centre located on our horizon." Cézanne's slow evolution, the result of a developing inner maturity, corresponds to the period from 1878 to 1895. This evolution was expressed particularly strongly in two motifs to which he returned again and again: the port of L'Estaque which he painted nineteen times in fifteen years, and the hilltop village of Gardanne, near Aix-en-Provence, whose landscape holds together as a single volume while its form gives the impression of a third dimension.

The great alliance between form and colour, a characteristic of Cézanne's maturity, is illustrated with rare magnificence in the paintings made at Jas de Bouffan, the country house his father owned near Aix. There, according to Roger Fry, one found "the struggle within him between the Baroque contortions and involutions with which his inner visions presented themselves to his mind, and the extreme simplicity, the Primitive or almost Byzantine interpretation which he gave naturally to the scenes of actual life." They recall the simplified patterns of the Primitives, allowing Guerry to compare Cézanne's use of space with that of the Siennese Primitives. Here one must understand this use of the word "primitive", for Cézanne's primitivism was the fruit of a patient work, an absolute simplification of vision as well as the result of long experience. This simplicity of the primitive was explained by Cézanne to Gasquet in these terms: "You can say what you like, but playing at ignorance and naiveté is the worst kind of decadence. Senility. Today one cannot help knowing things, learning by oneself. One breathes one's craft from birth." During this period Cézanne took up one of French art's classic themes, painted by such artists as Watteau, Boucher, Fragonard, Courbet and Renoir. It was that of bathers, a subject he had never abandoned; he had worked on the theme in one way or another for over thirty years. He also painted *Madame Cézanne with Loose Hair*, *Self-Portrait on a Blue Ground*, *Madame Cézanne in a Yellow Chair*, the extraordinary *Mardi-Gras* and his series of harlequins.

Woman with a Coffee Pot and *The Card Players* are transitional works, spanning two periods. The year 1895 was fertile for Cézanne. He painted more than three hundred canvases, most of which can be considered among his masterpieces. They were painted feverishly as a result of Cézanne's fear that he would not be able to finish his work before he died. Among them are seven self-portraits, eighteen paintings of his wife, three portraits of his son, twenty-one canvases of *Bathers*, four versions of *Boy in a Red Waistcoat*, fifty-four still-life paintings and the rest, landscapes. He worked tirelessly. One month before his death, he wrote to Emile Bernard: "I always study nature and it seems to me that I am making slow progress. I would have liked to have you here with me, for solitude always weighs a little heavy on me. But I am old and ill and I have sworn to die painting." Emile Zola's death in 1902 was a great shock to him. Even though their relationship had ended after the publication of Zola's work *L'Oeuvre*, the writer had been the great friend of Cézanne's youth.

In the last period of Cézanne's life, the pursuit of transparency and luminosity led him to a new interest in watercolours. He had worked with this medium throughout his life, but had previously used it mainly as a means for testing colours and forms. According to Dorival, "more vibrant and more spontaneous than oil paintings, yet still full of colour, watercolours were both true to nature and poetic. Because they were more suggestive and could be handled more freely, they responded perfectly to the demands of his genius." Cézanne especially liked to paint still lifes with watercolours. In *Dessert*, *Apples with a Jug and Bottle*, *Small Jug* and *Skull* and the superb *Garment Left on a Chair*, dating from 1900, the master from Aix attained the highest qualities of genuine "expressionism": breathing life into inert matter. In *Pines Shaken by the Wind* and *Pines at Bibemus*, he achieved a perfection in his watercolours that can be compared to that of Sung dynasty landscape painting from the eighth to the twelfth century. One thinks of the last words of the dying Goethe: "More light..." In his own intense response to light, Cézanne's final paintings were suffused with it.

1. Fishing Village at L'Estaque - c. 1870. Private collection - *"It's like a playing card", wrote Cézanne to Camille Pissarro of L'Estaque, the village of which he was so fond. His frank interpretation of the Provençal landscape in this canvas reveals an intensity of feeling and a relationship between space and volume that is measured and harmonious.*

2. Men Playing Bowls - 1872-75. Private collection, USA - *Around 1870 the artist left behind the romanticism of his previous work and entered a period of formal simplification. Following the advice of his friend Camille Pissarro, the painter lightened his palette; his figures, bathed in light, are rendered with broad strokes.*

3. Self-Portrait - c. 1880-81. Musée du Louvre, Paris - *The discipline of silence and isolation that Cézanne practised is evident in all his self-portraits. This one, painted towards his fortieth year, reveals an extraordinary energy along with a clear tendency towards abstraction and simplification.*

4. The Negro Scipio - 1866. Museu de Arte, São Paulo - *This work, which many consider the high point of Cézanne's romantic period, marks a transition from the visionary composition to a new expressionism. The static figure of the man is balanced by the nervous energy of the brushstrokes. The contrasts of pure colour laid on in bold thick strokes give the subject an aggressive freshness.*

5. Portrait of Madame Cézanne - 1872-77. Private collection - *Cézanne painted a number of portraits of his wife Hortense Fiquet who, apart from his mother, was the only woman in his life. The artist treated his portraits the same as his landscapes and still lifes; the cohesiveness between figure and objects is strict, with the motionless figure captured forever in its essence.*

6. Hanged Man's House - 1873. Musée d'Orsay, Paris - *This canvas, painted in Auvers-sur-Oise where Pissarro lived, is one of the first from Cézanne's Impressionist period and it is certainly among his best. One of the works he showed in 1874 at the first Impressionist exhibition held in the studio of the photographer Nadar, it was very poorly received by the public.*

7. The Bridge of Maincy - 1882-85. Musée du Louvre, Paris - *This is one of Cézanne's most famous landscapes. Note the importance he gave to geometric forms. Volume is rendered with fine brushstrokes, in green and blue tones, indicating the play of light and shadow.*

8. At the Jas de Bouffan - 1882-85. Private collection, USA - *Cézanne's father had a country house where the artist frequently went to paint outdoors. One can see in this work the artist's desire to construct and simplify the landscape with a kind of architectural synthesis.*

9. Zola's House at Médan - 1879-81. The Burrel Collection, Glasgow Art Gallery and Museum - *Cézanne went often to Médan to visit his childhood friend Zola, who moved there in 1878. This canvas, which originally belonged to Paul Gauguin, was painted with quick diagonal strokes building up to a kind of dynamic crescendo.*

10. The Poplars - 1879-82. Musée du Louvre, Paris - *Cézanne preferred to carry out his pictorial experiments with landscapes. He composed them by reducing forms to their essential lines and in this canvas he emphasised the vertical nature of the trees, which he considered true structural elements.*

11. A Modern Olympia - 1872-74. Musée d'Orsay, Paris - *During a visit to Auvers-sur-Oise with Dr. Gachet, Cézanne had an animated discussion with him about painting. The result was this canvas, full of brilliant and luminous colours which the master from Provence improvised in a clearly Impressionist style. Dr. Gachet was the first owner of the work.*

12. The Eternal Feminine - 1875-77. Private collection, USA - *This canvas dates from the same period as "A Modern Olympia" and has the same pyramid-like structure. This purely imaginative composition is in some ways visionary, yet if the fire of Romanticism is still apparent in the painting, the technique is nevertheless Impressionist.*

13. Nudes on the Shore - c. 1870. Private collection, France - *The two periods that Cézanne spent in Paris, in 1861 and in 1863, gave him the chance to meet the many artists gathered around Manet, the forerunner of the Impressionist movement. The techniques used for this watercolour give it great luminosity.*

14. Five Bathers - 1885-87. Kunstmuseum, Basle - *Using the same leitmotif as the previous work, this composition is centred around the female figures. They have been given monumental treatment by greatly simplifying them and arranging them in a balanced pyramid-like construction.*

15. Self-Portrait with Hat - 1879-82. Kunstmuseum, Bern - *Cézanne left seven self-portraits which reveal close personal observation as well as the painter's desire to abstract and to simplify. A tendency towards geometric analysis is evident in this self-portrait.*

16. Table Set for a Meal - 1875-76?. Private collection, USA - *This work was painted in Auvers-sur-Oise, near Pointoise, the home of Camille Pissarro, who had a strong influence on the painting of the master from Aix. Here, even though the brushwork is still heavy, the palette has become lighter and more luminous.*

17. Three Apples - c. 1872. Private collection - *Following the examples of the Dutch and Spanish schools, Cézanne, attentive to "the silent life of things", was attracted to familiar everyday objects. Perspective accentuates the structure of the volumes. Unlike the other Impressionists, his study of the effect of light on objects did not lead him to obliterate form but to exalt it.*

18. Still Life with Fruit and Pitcher - 1895-1900. Musée du Louvre, Paris - *This painting belongs to Cézanne's last period when his vision was fully realized. Taking a conventional subject, the artist has concentrated on technique to transform a material reality into a painterly reality.*

19. Still Life with Plaster Cupid - c. 1885. Courtauld Institute Gallery, London - *"There is no light or dark painting, there are only relationships of colour." This maxim of Cézanne's has been applied to this canvas where the structure and geometry of the work are created with the help of contrasts of colour.*

20. Plaster Cupid - c. 1895. National Museum, Stockholm - *Through the careful achievement of form the painter emphasised the volume of objects, which he defined through a simplification of contour lines. The different elements, carefully assembled, give energy to the whole.*

21. Madame Cézanne in the Conservatory - c. 1890. The Metropolitan Museum of Art, Stephen C. Clark Collection, New York - *Of the eighteen portraits Cézanne painted of his wife Hortense Fiquet, this is certainly the most famous. It belongs to Cézanne's period of pictorial synthesis when he attempted to blend abstraction with realism.*

22. Portrait of Madame Cézanne in Red - 1890-94. Museu de Arte, São Paulo - *Around 1890 Cézanne painted several portraits of his wife dressed in red. At the time he had abandoned the use of perspective in order to achieve a synthesis between the figure and the background, giving the image a monumental feeling.*

23. The Card Players - 1890-92. Musée d'Orsay, Paris - *Cézanne devoted five canvases to this theme, so dear to Caravaggio, turning it into a study of lines and volumes. The bottle, catching the light, divides the space into two symmetrical parts, and accentuates the contrast between the two players.*

24. The Reader - 1894-96. Private collection, USA - *This canvas was painted only ten years before Cézanne's death. During his last period, the function of the model took on ever greater importance in his works. The tragic element had long since disappeared from his portraits leaving in its place a sure use of geometry, softened by the choice of a natural pose.*

25. Portrait of Ambroise Vollard - 1899. Musée du Petit Palais, Paris - *In 1895 the painter displayed 150 paintings at the Rue Laffitte gallery of Ambroise Vollard, a collector and art dealer who would also write the first biography of Cézanne, rich in anecdotes. It was Cézanne's first exhibition in twenty years.*

26. Boy in a Red Waistcoat - 1890-95. Bührle Collection, Zurich - *There were four versions of this canvas portraying Michelangelo Di Rosa, a young Italian model. This work is certainly the best of the series because of the harmony of the boy's pose and the intensity of the colours.*

27. Man with a Pipe Leaning on a Table - 1895-1900. Kunsthalle, Mannheim - *Around 1895, the painter began to feel that he did not have much longer to live. As a result, he increased his efforts in a kind of creative fervour. He painted more than 300 works. Among them were many portraits in which he attempted to create a synthesis between the figure and the background.*

28. Seated Peasant - 1895-1900. Private collection, USA - *The sense of the tragic which fascinated the young Cézanne seems to have left his work completely. This famous painting from his last period presents a calmer vision of man but once more the individuality of the human figure is replaced by one that is more representative of the human figure in general.*

29. Old Woman with a Rosary - 1900-04. National Gallery, London - *The artist worked for eighteen months on this portrait. It reflects the sympathy Cézanne felt for people who "had grown old without doing violence to their customs as they gave themselves up to the laws of time."*

30. Harlequin - 1888-90. Private collection - *This work almost certainly portrays Cézanne's son Paul, dressed as a harlequin. The raised ground emphasises the volumes and space takes on precise forms. Cézanne's interest in the human figure is becoming more evident.*

31. Harlequin - 1888-90. Private collection, USA - *Like the previous work, this one belongs to a series of harlequins painted during the artist's last years, between 1900 and 1904. However, the period when Cézanne worked on them was too brief to consider it a genuine obsession. More likely the theme is connected to the French tradition of popular farce in the days of Le Nain (17th century).*

32. Nymphs by the Sea (left section) - 1890-94. Musée du Louvre (Orangerie), Paris - *This was a single painting that was cut into three parts. The centre section, portraying a boat, was subsequently lost. Commissioned by Choquet in 1888, it was intended to decorate his apartment. The painting, unfinished at the time of Choquet's death in 1891, was part of his collection sold in 1899.*

33. Nymphs by the Sea (right section) - 1890-94. Musée du Louvre (Orangerie), Paris - *During his last period, Cézanne showed a growing interest in the human figure and particularly in the leitmotif of bathers. He harmoniously balanced the dynamic vigour of the figures with the background to obtain a perfect synthesis of expression wherein the figures blend with the architecture of the landscape.*

34. Village Seen through Trees - c. 1885. Kunsthalle, Bremen - *Reality was the starting point for the imagination in many of Cézanne's paintings. Cézanne would begin with a a naturalistic subject that served as a basis for structural variants along abstract lines, and then would take the painting well beyond the point from which it started.*

35. Street Leading to a Lake - 1879-82. Kröller-Müller Museum, Otterlo - *From 1879 to 1882, Cézanne painted the motif of the winding road many times. He first began work on the theme in 1870, repeating it several times over the years.*

36. The Abandoned House - 1892-94. Private collection, USA - *In the landscapes of Cézanne's period of synthesis, the unity of the composition proceeded from a fluid and transparent fusion of colours. The canvas acquired a homogeneous solidity in which colour accentuated the force of the synthesis.*

37. Woods with Boulders - 1894-95. Kunsthaus, Zurich - *This is most likely a view of the forest of Fontainebleau but the actual location is not important because, according to Cézanne, "nature is always the same ... our art must make us appreciate it eternally."*

38. The Large Bathers - 1898-1905. Museum of Art, Philadelphia - *This work was considered the masterpiece of Cézanne's architectural compositions. The Arc, a little river that flows near Aix, served as background for the bathers. In the painting, forms and colours are diluted, giving the painting an Impressionist look, which, for Cézanne, was above all about construction.*

39. Woods at Château Noir - c. 1900. Musée du Louvre, Paris - *This work belongs to Cézanne's period of synthesis. The theme of trees tossed by the wind and treated as a structural unity, can be found throughout Cézanne's work.*

40. Mount Sainte-Victoire - 1904-06. Museum of Art, Philadelphia - *The artist's emotional ties to this landscape gave new meaning to the portrayal of objects. His vision of the thing imagined is recreated in a luminous and transparent representation.*

41. Mount Sainte-Victoire - 1904-06. Kunsthaus, Zurich - *In his last period Cézanne often left blank patches in his canvases. These empty spaces were not evidence of an inability to finish them. Rather they were transitional areas where two colours which could not be placed side by side faced each other and blended optically.*

42. Standing Female Nude - c. 1895. Musée du Louvre, Paris - *Painted at the same time as his harlequins, this watercolour over pencil sketch portrays the strong, solid woman that Cézanne habitually painted.*

43. Rooftops - c. 1904. Private collection, USA - *In his last years, Cézanne preferred to paint with watercolours because they allowed him to render light in a more immediate way. This did not in any way reduce the mastery of this oil on canvas painted two years before his death.*

44. Le Cabanon de Jourdan - 1906. Riccardo Jucker Collection, Milan - *Cézanne's famous phrase, proposing to treat nature according to the cylinder, the sphere and the cone with everything in proper perspective, which became the foundation of Cubism, is beautifully applied in this painting.*

1. *Fishing Village at L'Estaque* - c. 1870. Private collection

2. *Men Playing Bowls* - 1872-75. Private collection, USA

3. *Self-Portrait* - c. 1880-81. Musée du Louvre, Paris

4. *The Negro Scipio* - 1866. Museu de Arte, São Paulo

5. *Portrait of Madame Cézanne* - 1872-77. Private collection

6. *Hanged Man's House* - 1873. Musée d'Orsay, Paris

7. *The Bridge of Maincy* - 1882-85. Musée du Louvre, Paris

8. *At the Jas de Bouffan* - 1882-85. Private collection, USA

9. *Zola's House at Médan* - 1879-81. The Burrel Collection, Glasgow Art Gallery and Museum

10. *The Poplars* - 1879-82. Musée du Louvre, Paris

11. *A Modern Olympia* - 1872-74. Musée d'Orsay, Paris

12. *The Eternal Feminine* - 1875-77. Private collection, USA

13. *Nudes on the Shore* - c. 1870. Private collection, France

14. *Five Bathers* - 1885-87. Kunstmuseum, Basle

15. *Self-Portrait with Hat* - 1879-82. Kunstmuseum, Bern

16. *Table Set for a Meal* - 1875-76?. Private collection, USA

17. *Three Apples* - c. 1872. Private collection

18. *Still Life with Fruit and Pitcher* - 1895-1900. Musée du Louvre, Paris

19. *Still Life with Plaster Cupid* - c. 1885. Courtauld Institute Gallery, London

20. *Plaster Cupid* - c. 1895. National Museum, Stockholm

21. *Madame Cézanne in the Conservatory* - c. 1890. The Metropolitan Museum of Art, Stephen C. Clark Collection, New York

22. *Portrait of Madame Cézanne in Red* - 1890-94. Museu de Arte, São Paulo

23. *The Card Players* - 1890-92. Musée d'Orsay, Paris

24. *The Reader* - 1894-96. Private collection, USA

25. *Portrait of Ambroise Vollard* - 1899. Musée du Petit Palais, Paris

27. *Man with a Pipe Leaning on a Table* - 1895-1900. Kunsthalle, Mannheim

26. *Boy in a Red Waistcoat* - 1890-95. Bührle Collection, Zurich

28. *Seated Peasant* - 1895-1900. Private collection, USA

29. *Old Woman with a Rosary* - 1900-04. National Gallery, London

30. *Harlequin* - 1888-90. Private collection

31. *Harlequin* - 1888-90. Private collection, USA

32. *Nymphs by the Sea* (left section) - 1890-94. Musée du Louvre (Orangerie), Paris

33. *Nymphs by the Sea* (right section) - 1890-94. Musée du Louvre (Orangerie), Paris

34. *Village Seen through Trees* - c. 1885. Kunsthalle, Bremen

35. *Street Leading to a Lake* - 1879-82. Kröller-Müller Museum, Otterlo

36. *The Abandoned House* - 1892-94. Private collection, USA

37. *Woods with Boulders* - 1894-95. Kunsthaus, Zurich

38. *The Large Bathers* - 1898-1905. Museum of Art, Philadelphia

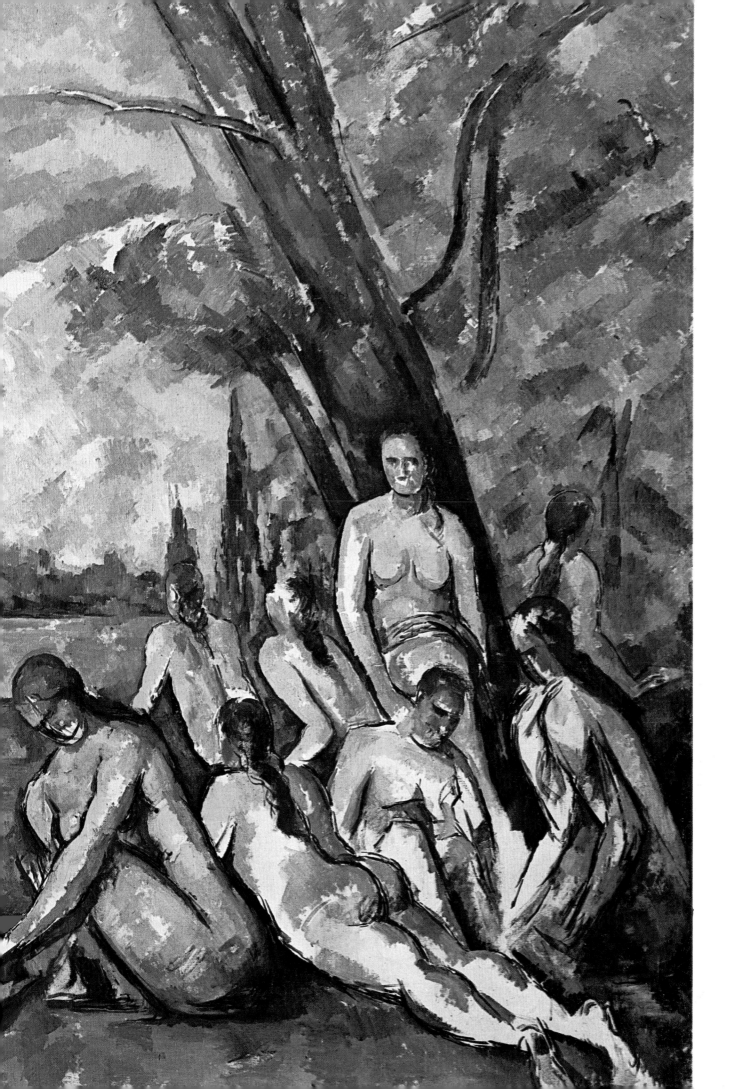

39. *Woods at Château Noir* - c. 1900. Musée du Louvre, Paris

40. *Mount Sainte-Victoire* - 1904-06. Museum of Art, Philadelphia

41. *Mount Sainte-Victoire* - 1904-06. Kunsthaus, Zurich

42. *Standing Female Nude* - c. 1895. Musée du Louvre, Paris

43. *Rooftops* - c. 1904. Private collection, USA

44. *Le Cabanon de Jourdan* - 1906. Riccardo Jucker Collection, Milan

Editor in chief Anna Maria Mascheroni

Art director Luciano Raimondi

Text Alberta Melanotte

Translation Kerry Milis

Production Art, Bologna

Photo Credits Gruppo Editoriale Fabbri S.p.A., Milan

Copyright © 1988 by Gruppo Editoriale S.p.A., Milan

Published by Park Lane
An imprint of Books & Toys Limited
The Grange
Grange Yard
LONDON
SE1 3AG

ISBN 1-85627-185-4

This edition published 1991

Printed in Italy by Gruppo Editoriale Fabbri S.p.A., Milan